starving

tosh l. brown

Expand Knowledge Publications
www.expandknowledge.net

ISBN: 978-0-6152-1816-8

INTRODUCTION

"Starving," consist of selected journal writings, inspired by many circumstances in my life, individuals who have crossed my path, and God's revelation to me. Though the book was written about four years ago, it has been a nine-year journey. The scripture references were put on my heart in the past year. The purpose of the scripture is to share answers to my thoughts and unanswered questions. I believe God determines the perfect timing as to when to present a gift to another.

"Think big…start small." My goal for writing this book was not to be full of myself; instead, my goal is that at least one person would be impacted for Christ as a result of reading some of my thoughts. Initially I feared being labeled all sorts of things and being placed in a box. I had to allow God to show me who I am in Him. I pray that all who read this book allow God to speak to them, through my little thoughts and me. Enjoy!!!

-Tosh

ABOUT THE AUTHOR

A native of San Diego, California, Ms. Brown has been residing in the Prince Georges County area for the past nine years. Ms. Brown encourages others through her day-to-day interactions with students, and clients of **Lainifu's Touch**, her recently launched errand service business. She has had the pleasure of writing for her previous employer and for church newsletters.

If you enjoyed the book and would like to provide feedback, email Ms. Brown at toshb1074@yahoo.com.

SPECIAL THANKS

I would like to thank GOD, for without HIM this would not have been possible.

To my Mom for being my biggest cheerleader, my Dad for introducing me to Strunk.

Special thanks to my good friend CJ who encouraged me to write this book 10 years ago.

Thanks to the Brown, Lewis, Blevins, and Sharpe families, my Queen Esther Sisters from First Baptist of Glenarden, the Bayview Baptist Family, and the Messiah Lutheran Family.

I would especially like to thank all of my dream killers....you are the best!!!

TABLE OF CONTENTS

TABLE OF CONTENTS

THE MEAL:
FINANCIAL PORTFOLIO

It is important to understand your worth; even more important is what you deposit into your soul. You are more valuable than anything that monetary sources can bring. In my adolescent years I measured my net worth by the approval and disapproval of my peers. As I transitioned into my twenties, I crossed the path of a licensed spiritual doctor, who brought to my attention the blindsided vision of my worth and buying power. My twenties were the years of proving, pursuing, and paying. I was proving that I could get my worth, pursuing worth, and paying the price for worth that was and is not worth.

It is unfortunate that at that age, I did not recognize how much buying power I had, due to my gross worth. Worth is a beautiful thing! In society, images of lifestyles state; the more worth, the better. I translate that as the more I invest in me, the better my life will become. You are like an account. If you deposit into you, your worth grows. The challenging part is making the decision of what to deposit, hold, clear, and withdrawal from your account. Negative balances are not good for your soul. Bouncing checks are like depositing negative energy or holding on.

Mark 4:31-32 – It is like a mustard seed which, when it is sown on the ground, is smaller than all the seeds on earth; but when it is sown, it grows up and becomes greater than all herbs, and shoots out large branches, so that the birds of the air may nest under its shade.

Mark 12:41-44 – Now Jesus sat opposite the treasury and saw how the people put money into the treasury. And many who were rich put in much. Then one poor widow came and threw in two mites, which make a quadrans.

So He called His disciples to Himself and said to them, Assuredly, I say to you that this poor widow has put in more than all those who have given to the treasury; for they all put in out of their abundance, but she out of her poverty put in all that she had, her whole livelihood.

THE MEAL:
COMPLIMENTARY CRITICISM

For every compliment one receives, a bashing awaits. It is great to receive praise for a job well done or just for you being yourself. Is it great to receive a little bashing from those who do not praise your being? At one time in my life I would say, "No!" Today, I believe both types of criticism are good for the soul. Praises are well received and criticism is often a hard pill to swallow, yet, criticism is great food for the soul.

Criticism encourages me to become a better person. I now understand that it is to enhance my growth. Without criticism, one will not know where they may want to brush up on the canvas, tighten a few nuts and bolts. One can gain plenty of inner strength through praise and criticism at the same time. If one is continuously being praised, their growth may be stunted. Throw a little haterade to rev up their engine. So whenever you receive a compliment, practice embracing the criticism that will follow. It is not being pessimistic; it is facing truth, which has to take place, so you will not stop growing.

Proverbs 8:17- I love those who love me, and those who seek me diligently will find me.

Proverbs 12:2- A good man obtains favor from the LORD, but a man of wicked intentions He will condemn.

Proverbs 15:32- He who disdains instruction despises his own soul, but he who heeds rebuke gets understanding.

Proverbs 27:2, 5- Let another man praise you and not your own mouth; A stranger and not your own lips. Open rebuke is better than love carefully concealed.

Matthew 18:7 – Woe to the world because of offenses! For offenses must come, but woe to the man by whom the offense comes!

Psalm 119:71 – It is good for me that I have been afflicted, that I may learn Your statutes.

Romans 12:14 - Bless those who persecute you; bless and do not curse.

THE MEAL:
GIVING WITH THOUGHT

Practice giving more. Practice being a silent giver. Giving aloud may be misinterpreted for something else. One will always assume there is a reason for giving. The reason is, <u>you can!</u> You can give in so many ways. Give love, a smile, a hug, a card, a greeting, a goodbye, a listening ear, a phone call, a compliment, and most of all, give TIME. These are some of the best gifts one can give.

It is amazing, how many individuals have never received those gifts. Giving should definitely come from the heart. In the past I have given things expecting a "Thank you," or consideration for my actions. My feelings have been hurt. I had to go back to my core purpose; give, because I have been given so much. It is in my heart.

Matthew 6: 1-4

Proverbs 22:9- He who has a generous eye will be blessed, for he gives of his bread to the poor.

Proverbs 3:27 – Do not withhold good from those to whom it is due, when it is in the power of your hand to do so.

Proverbs 28:14 – Happy is the man who is always reverent, but he who hardens his heart will fall into calamity.

Proverbs 21:14 – A gift in secret pacifies anger, and a bribe behind the back, strong wrath.

Acts 20:35 – "I have shown you in every way, by laboring like this , that you must support the weak, and remember the words of the Lord Jesus, that He said; " It is more blessed to give than to receive."

Colossians 3:17- And whatever you do in word or deed, do all in the name of the Lord Jesus, giving thanks to God the Father through him.

Additional servings:
Deuteronomy 15:10-11, 15

THE MEAL:
OKAY

It is okay. That is key to enduring any challenge, setback, heartache or general life experience. *It is okay*. Everything always turns out, with defining results. People become anxious and uneasy when they can not foresee or control the outcome in situations. No matter whether it is considered good or bad, *it is okay*.

As I read this, I know it is important for me to believe and trust that whatever is to come, *it will be okay*. That is hard to bear when one has lost someone or something valuable. *Keep trying! Never give up! It is okay. Change the frown. Why is your head down? You are okay. I won!!! I passed the test. Today, I know it is okay.*

Philippians 4:6 – Be anxious for nothing, but in everything by prayer and supplication, with thanksgiving, let your request be made known to God

Psalm 48:14 – For this is God, Our God forever and ever; He will be our guide even to death.

Psalm 62:5 – My soul, wait silently for God alone, for my expectation is from Him.

Psalm 138:7 – Though I walk in the midst of trouble, you will revive me; you will stretch out your hand against the wrath of the enemies, and your right hand will save me

Additional servings:
Psalm 40:1-3
Psalm 61:1-8

THE MEAL:
LIFE CHOICE

Choose life! There are incidents that occur in one's life. The condition can place thoughts in the mind to give up on a goal, a hobby, a person, or fighting a life changing illness. One does not want to move forward. They may choose to mentally or physically handicap themselves from perseverance.

Choose life! In the past I have gone through challenges that appear to be negative and a dark cloud. I did not want to move forward, *because that was a feeling.* As divine intervention had its way, it was soon revealed that *I wanted life*. Life has a lot to offer. When we all leave this earth, a few of us think we will end up in another place. Wherever you go, chances are you will be allowed to reflect on what you did on earth. Ask yourself. *Through it all, did I choose to live my life?*

Psalm 119:50 – This is my comfort in my affliction, for your word has given me life.

Romans 14:12- So then each of us shall give account to himself to God.

Additional serving:
Psalm 63:1-8

THE MEAL:
LAW ABIDING

Strive to do the right thing. Doing the right thing in life pays off in the end. It will benefit other people. As an adult who stands before children on a daily basis, I have a responsibility. I am responsible to myself and to these children to do what is right. One cannot assume that they know what is doing right. What may be morally right or politically correct could be taught that it is wrong in their culture, family, and environment.

It is good to show others. Eventually others may emulate doing the right thing, because they saw you or I do right. Also, there will come a time where you will have to answer to someone. We are accountable for everything we do. I personally would like to be known as *the person who followed through* on doing right, even if the condition, action, or circumstance is wrong.

Psalms

119:33-40 - HE. Teach me, O LORD, the way of thy statutes; and I shall keep it unto the end. Give me understanding, and I shall keep thy law; yea, I shall observe it with my whole heart. Make me to go in the path of thy commandments; for therein do I delight. Incline my heart unto thy testimonies, and not to covetousness. Turn away mine eyes from beholding vanity; and quicken thou me in thy way. Stablish thy word unto thy servant, who is devoted to thy fear. Turn away my reproach which I fear: for thy judgments are good. Behold, I have longed after thy precepts: quicken me in thy righteousness.

19:21 – There are many plans in a man's heart, nevertheless the Lord's counsel- that will stand.

20:11- Even a child is known by his deeds, whether what he does is pure and right.

21:21-He who follows righteousness and mercy finds life, righteousness and honor.

21:2-3 Every way of a man is right in his own eyes, but the Lord weighs the hearts; To do righteousness and justice is more acceptable to the Lord than sacrifice.

22:6- Train up a child in the way he should go, and when he is old he will not depart from it.

THE MEAL:
ACCEPTING

Acceptance is the main ingredient sought in our own recipe of life. It is thought that without acceptance, our life is not as fulfilled or truly given recognition deserve, with out the notary of an acceptance stamp all over it. You cannot use any form of payment aside from cash, unless the screen shows approved. On every application the word acceptance appears. We receive acceptance letters, accept calls, accept offer, accept invites, etc.

It is amazing how one term dictates our moves on a day-to-day basis. We even make acceptance speeches. We want to be accepted based on our education, where we live, our careers, our attire, social environment, our income, culture, God-given features, and changed features. All this is done in vain of receiving that word from society.

We need to seek that word from self, first. I believe once that takes place, our mission in life will be different. Or our motivating force will bring about wisdom in accomplishing the goal.

Luke 18:17 – Assuredly, I say to you, whoever does not receive the kingdom of God as a little child will by no means enter it.

Roman 1:5 - Through him we have received grace and apostleship for obedience to the faith among all nations for his name.

8:5 - For those who live according to the flesh set their minds on the things of the flesh, but those who live according to the Spirit, the things of the Spirit.

9:8 – That is those who are the children of the flesh, these are not the children of God; but the children of the promise are counted as the seed.

10:3 - For they being ignorant of God's righteousness, and seeking to establish their own righteousness, have not submitted to the righteousness of God.

Additional servings:
1 Corinthians 15:58
Colossians 2:10
1 Timothy 2:3-4

THE MEAL:
PRISONER RELEASED

Release self from old ways or habits that are not beneficial to your well-being. If your end result is negative, practice or strive to do the extreme opposite. This is a task that takes a lifetime to master. One should start with small ways or habits that can make your life or circumstance better. With each habit, write it down. Ask self the purpose for habits in life.

What are the advantages and disadvantages of holding on to this habit? *Can you see the rewards of releasing this habit?* The goal is to conquer. Some of us prefer to be the victim of defeat. It is important to practice realistic steps to giving up a habit. Like a New Year's Resolution, we write a list of things to do, and normally cannot accomplish the top five. The reason being is that we were not being realistic and honest with ourselves.

During the holiday season, more than enough of my old habits and iniquities jumped out to the surface. I battled internally and externally with self. It took place in silence. My physical stance spoke loud and clear. I had *to ask self, how would this benefit me?* As I coached myself through prayer, I knew I could release the old way or habit.

We should all find a way to help release self from old habits seek someone you can talk to, exercise, meditate, pray, etc. Hopefully whatever assistance or new habit you obtain will be beneficial to you and those you interact with.

2 Corinthians 2:10 - To whom ye forgive any thing, I forgive also: for if I forgave any thing, to whom I forgave it, for your sakes forgave I it in the person of Christ;

Ephesians 6:11-13 - Put on the whole armour of God, that ye may be able to stand against the wiles of the devil. For we wrestle not against flesh and blood, but against principalities, against powers, against the rulers of the darkness of this world, against spiritual wickedness in high places. Wherefore take unto you the whole armour of God, that ye may be able to withstand in the evil day, and having done all, to stand.

Colossians 3:5 -Mortify therefore your members which are upon the earth; fornication, uncleanness, inordinate affection, evil concupiscence, and covetousness, which is idolatry:

Change Mindset

I am trying to let go.
I will let go.
I have let go.
Gone!
-Colossians 3:2

THE MEAL:
FOCUS FOR TODAY

Today, I feel content and at peace. I am where I need to be. If the feeling of being uncertain comes up, I must check in the past or archives of what steps and events have placed me where I am today. A week ago today, I did not feel what I feel this very moment. I can now reflect on that day. I was in the setting of unwavering spirits. To their defense, those spirits did not know once it came to me what had taken place. I became determined to seek solace. *Give thanks for who you are and where you are. It is sad, how we take things for granted. We are normally better off than we know. Appreciate what you have. Where would you be right now, if you did not have?*

1 Corinthians 7:17 – But as God has distributed to each one, the Lord has called each one, so let him walk, and so I ordain in all the churches.

1 Corinthians 7:20 – Let each one remain in the same calling in which he was called.

1 Timothy 6:6 – Now godliness with contentment is great gain.

Colossians 3:2 – Set your mind on things above, not on things on the earth.

Philippians 1:19- For I know that this will turn out for my deliverance through your prayer and the supply of the Spirit of Jesus Christ.

Additional serving:
1 Thessalonians 4:11-12.

THE MEAL:
UNDERSTANDING

Be open to understanding. It provides insight. Understanding reveals that one cares. Wanting to understand shows maturity, healing, objectivity, and love. Understanding brings forth balance and competence. Understanding the will of life brings purpose. Make it a goal to understand today.

Proverb 19:8- He who gets wisdom loves his own soul; he who keeps understanding will find good.

28:2- Because of transgression of a land, may are princes; but by a man of understanding and knowledge, right will be prolonged.

THE MEAL:
WILLING WORKS

Be willing to do what it takes to get what is needed. Most individuals do not want to do what it takes. Why is that? What is holding one back? Fear? Disability? Lack of desire? Everyday, we watch reality television shows, where people of all walks of life display their weakness and strengths, to be ridiculed by strangers to get what they want. This all happens because they are willing. I thought, "If I am not willing to do what it takes to get what I need then how can I encourage or suggest to others to do what I have not been willing to do myself?"

1 Peter 4:1- Therefore, since Christ suffered for us in the flesh, arm yourselves also with the same mind, for he who has suffered in the flesh has ceased from sin.

THE MEAL:
CULTURAL COMPETENCE

No matter the race, gender, age, or socioeconomic status, we can all learn from one another. I try to receive all encounters with new and old acquaintances, as a moment to learn. It is unfortunate that in today's society, we are still taught not to engage with certain persons or groups. I believe if a person is not intended to harm you emotionally or physically, you should be able to associate with them.

Sometimes the encounter only involves listening. Listen to the history; process your personality as well as the other person's personality. Listen to make sense of a other's viewpoint. In life we all follow some belief system, which allows us to have balance, peace, love, and understanding. My belief is in God and the Bible. Contrary to what society believes about the Bible, most books follow the principles of the Bible. Although it is unrecognized, due to other jargon being used.

Colossians 2:2 –that their hearts maybe encouraged, being knit together in love, and attaining, to all riches of the full assurance of understanding, to the knowledge of the mystery of God, both of the father and the Christ.

THE MEAL:
SELF-EVALUATION

Be honest with self. This is the key to healing. When a person becomes honest without justification, they are one step closer to the road of success. Honesty can hurt or heal. Honesty can bring out a jovial heart or jaded spirit. Honesty will reveal faith or fear. Honesty can open the door to your future. Honesty can shut the door to your past. If the goal is to move forward and be victorious in your life, *ALWAYS BE HONEST!*

Psalm 51

1 Have mercy upon me, O God, according to thy lovingkindness: according unto the multitude of thy tender mercies blot out my transgressions. 2 Wash me throughly from mine iniquity, and cleanse me from my sin. 3 For I acknowledge my transgressions: and my sin is ever before me. 4 Against thee, thee only, have I sinned, and done this evil in thy sight: that thou mightest be justified when thou speakest, and be clear when thou judgest. 5 Behold, I was shapen in iniquity; and in sin did my mother conceive me. 6 Behold, thou desirest truth in the inward parts: and in the hidden part thou shalt make me to know wisdom.

7 Purge me with hyssop, and I shall be clean: wash me, and I shall be whiter than snow. 8 Make me to hear joy and gladness; that the bones which thou hast broken may rejoice. 9 Hide thy face from my sins, and blot out all mine iniquities. 10 Create in me a clean heart, O God; and renew a right spirit within me. 11 Cast me not away from thy presence; and take not thy holy spirit from me. 12 Restore unto me the joy of thy salvation; and uphold me with thy free spirit. 13 Then will I teach transgressors thy ways; and sinners shall be converted unto thee.

14 Deliver me from bloodguiltiness, O God, thou God of my salvation: and my tongue shall sing aloud of thy righteousness. 15 O Lord, open thou my lips; and my mouth shall shew forth thy praise. 16 For thou desirest not sacrifice; else would I give it: thou delightest not in burnt offering. 17 The sacrifices of God are a broken spirit: a broken and a contrite heart, O God, thou wilt not despise. 18 Do good in thy good pleasure unto Zion: build thou the walls of Jerusalem. 19 Then shalt thou be pleased with the sacrifices of righteousness, with burnt offering and whole burnt offering: then shall they offer bullocks upon thine altar.

THE MEAL:
WEAKNESS STRENGTHEN

Strive to do whatever it is that annoys you or what you find difficult to do. It could be exercise, drinking water, eating right, reading, being kind to the unkind, time management, obtaining employment, maintaining employment, or even smiling. So many people find these things difficult to do. I am sure if we all would attempt to tackle one of our difficult tasks, we would see our lifestyle changed for the better. Practice putting effort in doing the things that you do not want to do. It always pays off.

Ecclesiastes 8: 16-18 – When I applied my heart to know wisdom and to see the business that is done on earth, even though one sees no sleep day or night, then I saw all the work of God, that a man cannot find out the work that is done under the sun. For though a man labors to discover it, yet he will not find it; moreover, though a wise man attempts to know it, he will not be able to find it.

THE MEAL:
VOICES HEARD

Your inner voice speaks loud and clear. Your inner voice reveals the root of you. Listen to your inner voice. What is the voice saying? Hearing fear? Insecurity? Uncertainty? When you hear your inner voice, are you able to rationalize the nurturing of that voice? Do you believe that inner voice? In life if we are in an environment where a person is continuously, given negative feedback, it is easy for the inner voice to repeat it over and over until the voice sounds natural. There is an inner voice that is opposite. This voice speaks affirmations, it is encouraging, and this voice is conscientious of what other inner voice is not beneficial.

Psalm 3:4 - I cried to the Lord with my voice, and He heard me from His holy hill.

Psalm 5:1 – Give ear to my words, O Lord. Consider my meditation.

Psalm 12:6 – The words of the Lord are pure words, Like silver tried in a furnace of earth, Purified seven times.

Psalm 14:1 – The fool has said in his heart, "There is no God" They are corrupt they have done abominable works, There is none who is good.

THE MEAL:
DETERMINATION

Determination is a great asset. This reveals your intention, your focus, your willpower, and your sacrifices. Determined individuals always succeed in their plight. So be determined to enhance not only your life, but all who come in contact with you. Be determined for a good cause.

Proverbs 13:12 - Hope deferred makes the heart sick, but when the desire comes, it is a tree of life.

THE MEAL:
OUT OF YOUR CONTROL

When it is out of your control, HOPE for the best. THINK of positive outcomes.

It is important to realize that most circumstance occur to release self from the desire to control. It is great to seek the best, prepare for the best, and with all your might be your best, though in the end what will happen is truly out of your control.

Although being passionate, giving the right response, displaying the appropriate actions, and having pure motives from the heart may receive recognition; in the end it is out of your control. So, as you move on in life and have delays and accomplishments, please remember, it is out of your control.

Genesis 6:8- But Noah found grace in the eyes of the Lord.

Additional serving:
Joshua 1:6-9

THE MEAL:
POSITIVE THINKING/ HAVING FAITH

Have you ever found it difficult to think positive in an uncertain situation? When highs turn low? When good turns bad? Maybe you are in a negative environment? We know it is easier said than done. If you think positive, believe with a positive attitude, your outcome will be the most positive suited response according to the circumstance. Having faith is another way to practice thinking positive. Faith believes for the best outcome. It is knowing, that no matter what hand is dealt to you, if you have the faith it will all work it self out.

Opportunity will arise to go against what you have faith in or are thinking positive for. This may actually be a roadblock. Practice waiting out your options before choosing the roadblock. You may find that sticking with your faith and positive thinking may lead to the true reward you are seeking.

Luke 17:6 – So the Lord said. "If you have faith as a mustard seed, you can say to this mulberry tree, Be pulled up by the roots and be planted in the sea, and it would obey it.

Additional servings:
Romans 5:2-11
Hebrew 11
1 Peter 1:6-9

THE MEAL:
APPRECIATING PROPERTY VALUE

Appreciate where you are this very moment. Know that there is someone else in a more unsettling situation than you are. Appreciate what you have. It is not always good to wish to be in another person or in another place. Appreciate your employment, the roof over the head, the meals you have today, the same clothes that are yours, your children, your spouse or significant other, and especially the parent or guardian that is still alive. Appreciate the transportation that you mistreat and take for granted. Appreciate the disappointments in your life. Appreciate all of life's experiences. Appreciate yourself.

Society tells us to want more, trade that in, and do this. Society should display appreciation in lifestyles. It is important to appreciate whatever you have. If you are unappreciative for a thing or person, it will be hard to appreciate the next. Try not to wait and lose out on all. If you appreciate the small, you can appreciate the large. Appreciate the hard times, so you can appreciate the good times. All appreciation is defining moments of what is true in your heart.

If you appreciate, you will not depreciate.

2 Corinthians 12:7-9 - And lest I should be exalted above measure through the abundance of the revelations, there was given to
me a thorn in the flesh, the messenger of Satan to buffet me, lest I
should be exalted above measure. 8 For this thing I besought the
Lord thrice, that it might depart from me. 9 And he said unto me,
My grace is sufficient for thee: for my strength is made perfect in
weakness. Most gladly therefore will I rather glory in my infirmi-
ties, that the power of Christ may rest upon me.

2 Peter 1: 3-7 - According as his divine power hath given unto us
all things that pertain unto life and godliness, through the knowledge of him that hath called us to glory and virtue: 4 Whereby
are given unto us exceeding great and precious promises: that by
these ye might be partakers of the divine nature, having escaped
the corruption that is in the world through lust.

5 And beside this, giving all diligence, add to your faith virtue;
and to virtue knowledge; 6 And to knowledge temperance; and to
temperance patience; and to patience godliness; 7 And to godliness brotherly kindness; and to brotherly kindness charity.

THE MEAL: SERVE

Serving people is not an easy job. When you serve people out of joy, it is rewarding. When you serve people out of obligation, your attitude may not be as pleasant. It is important to remember that serving others is a choice.

When you are in the position to be served, it is that individual's choice to serve you. If by chance you are in the position to serve, treat them as if you were serving yourself. Knowing you, how would you like to be served?

Galatians 5:13-For you brethren, have been called to liberty; only do not use liberty as an opportunity for the flesh, but through love serve one another.

Proverbs 21:13-Whoever shuts his ear to cry of the poor will also cry himself and not be heard.

22:29- Do you see a man who excels in his work: He will stand before kings; hew will not stand before unknown men.
James 3:18-Now the fruit of the righteousness is sown in peace by those who make peace.

2 John 1:6- This is love that we walk according to his commandments; This is a commandment, that as you have heard from the beginning, you should walk in it.

Additional serving:
Matthew 20:20-28

THE MEAL:
BE

Be

Be the best
Be your best
Be what brings joy to others
Be what brings out the good in you
Be there for those who need you
Be of support
Be where there is peace
Be in love
Be of love
Be a friend
Be a parent
Be a child
Be a spouse
Be important
Be a teacher
Be a healer
Be a guide
Be human
Be you

Ecclesiastes 9:10 - Whatever your hand finds to do, do it with your might; for there is no work or device or knowledge or wisdom in the grave where you are going.

THE MEAL:
REFLECTION

Here you go again, what has kept you going? Is it the power? Money? Love? People? As you make this round, has the goal been accomplished? Has the purpose been served? Are you sticking to what you set out to do? By doing this, are you helping someone else other than yourself? After this, will you finally be satisfied? So do you really have to do this or are you just continuing to tell yourself that you have to? We can justify all of our actions, all day long. What would be pleasing in the sight of God? All of these thoughts while looking in the mirror.

Ecclesiastes 4:4&8;-Again I saw that fro all toil and every skillful work a man is envied by his neighbor. This also is vanity and grasping for the wind.

- There is one alone, without companion: He has neither son nor brother; Yet there is no end to all his labors, nor is his eye satisfied with riches. But he never asks, for whom do I toil and deprive myself of good? This also is vanity and a grave misfortune.

Proverbs 27:19- As In water face reflects face, so a man's heart reveals the man.

THE MEAL:
CHANGING FACES

What is the first step to change? I believe it is acknowledging there is a need. You also must make a decision to change. In order for change, one must be a willing participant. What are the perceptions of the outcome involving change: Perception plays a key role. Not all of us are open, flexible, and receptive to information to enhance the progression of change. Change is a temporary scar for healing wounds permanently.

Philippians 4:13 – I can do all things through Christ who strengthens me

THE MEAL:
A DEFINING MOMENT

A defining moment occurs at the very second a lesson is learned, a revelation revealed, or a mission accomplished. Defining moments can persuade an individual to move forward, stand still, or take a step back. Where have your defining moments lead you?

Psalm 119:100 – I understand more than the ancients, Because I keep your Precepts.

THE MEAL:
THE GOOD LIFE ... PART 1

Life is good! I do not have a lot of material possessions. Life is good!

I have not traveled around the world. Life is still good! I have not acquired degrees and recognition. My life is good! To those looking from the outside, they may have formed their own opinions, saying, "Poor ole'….., she just has the worst luck." I would say, "Yes, that did happen to me. My life is so good!" It has been said repeatedly, it is not what occurred, but how you respond to what occurred. I see life as good. I will continue to have the serendipity outlook. How will you see your life?

1 Peter 1:6 - Wherein ye greatly rejoice, though now for a season, if need be, ye are in heaviness through manifold temptations

1 Peter 4:14 - If ye be reproached for the name of Christ, happy are ye; for the spirit of glory and of God resteth upon you: on their part he is evil spoken of, but on your part he is glorified.

Additional serving:
Psalms 84: 5-8

THE MEAL:
THE GOOD LIFE ... PART 2

My family cannot help me. Life is good! I have no money. Life is good! I have no home of my own. My life is good! Everyone else is always first. It is okay, my life is good! I will have to drop out. Life is good! I have never….. Life is good! My heart is broken. Life is good! I am in debt. My life is good! It is going to take a long time to recover. Through it all, LIFE IS GOOD!

Philippians 4:11, 4:19 - Not that I speak in respect of want: for I have learned, in whatsoever state I am, therewith to be content.

19 But my God shall supply all your need according to his riches in glory by Christ Jesus.

1 Thessalonians 5:16 - Rejoice evermore.

THE MEAL: TALENTS

Use your talent or gift to change the way a person may view the way of life. Your gift may show that there are other options. These options can be to enhance their well-being. The way of life for some is not the American Dream. In reality, everyone has a gift or talent of some sort. Some of us use ours as soon as we recognize what it is. There is nothing wrong with using your gift or talent to help others recognize their own, or to encourage others to use their gifts and talents to fulfill their destiny. By doing this, more American dreams will become an American reality.

James 4:17 - Therefore to him that knoweth to do good, and doeth it not, to him it is sin.

Romans 1:5 - By whom we have received grace and apostleship, for obedience to the faith among all nations, for his name

Additional serving:
Matthew 25: 14-30

.

THE MEAL:
COOKING (SOWING SEED)

It is time to cook. Cook whatever you would like. When you cook, there is normally a desire and a purpose. You have to have the required resources to cook. You have to be in a certain place and have the right temperature. When you allot time for cooking, you are responsible for what is being cooked. It is okay to have assistance. If you followed the recipe or cooking wisdom, what you cook will leave a savoring taste. All those who are feed, will return for more helpings. If you are not cooking, ask yourself why not? If you are cooking, are you putting in the right ingredients?

Matthew 7: 15-29

Matthew 12:33 - Either make the tree good, and his fruit good; or else make the tree corrupt, and his fruit corrupt: for the tree is known by his fruit.

2 Corinthians 9:6- But this I say: He who sows sparingly will also reap sparingly, and he who sows bountifully will also reap bountifully.

2 Corinthians 9:10- Now may he who supplies seed to the sower, and bread for food, supply and multiply the seed you have sown and increase the fruits of your righteousness.

THE MEAL:
FULL

After we have had enough to eat we say, "Whoa, I am full!" Being full can represent so many things. One can be full of good and evil. You can be full of love or hate. There are over the counter drugs sold in society, for a person to take so they will have the feeling of being full. There are also side effects to go with this feeling as well. A person can consume too much of something. Depending on what we fill ourselves up with, determines the length of our side effects. Ask yourself, what do I want to be full of?

Proverbs 25:16 - Hast thou found honey? eat so much as is sufficient for thee, lest thou be filled therewith, and vomit it.

1 Peter 1:2-3 - Elect according to the foreknowledge of God the Father, through sanctification of the Spirit, unto obedience and sprinkling of the blood of Jesus Christ: Grace unto you, and peace, be multiplied.

3 Blessed be the God and Father of our Lord Jesus Christ, which according to his abundant mercy hath begotten us again unto a lively hope by the resurrection of Jesus Christ from the dead,

1 Peter 3:8 - Finally, be ye all of one mind, having compassion one of another, love as brethren, be pitiful, be courteous

THE MEAL:
OCCURRENCE

Have you ever had an encounter where you are in your own space, at peace? Then suddenly you are blindsided when someone close to you says something intended to hurt you. They may even secretly just want you to react in a negative fashion. Before you know it, mission accomplished. What are you to do? Make a decision that very moment, to focus on yourself and the role you play in the outcome. Of course it seems easier to just lash out. What you will normally find in the end, is that it has nothing to do with you.

As much as you want to let that person have it, for ruining your good space, give yourself time to put it all in perspective. It may be that person's issue. You were just chosen to partake in the matter. Embrace the situation and say, "Hey, I will learn and grow from this." It is hard. You will get through this and make the right decision.

2 Corinthians 2:5-11 - But if any have caused grief, he hath not grieved me, but in part: that I may not overcharge you all.

6 Sufficient to such a man is this punishment, which was inflicted of many.

7 So that on the contrary ye ought rather to forgive him, and comfort him, lest perhaps such a one should be swallowed up with overmuch sorrow.

8 Wherefore I beseech you that ye would confirm your love toward him.

9 For to this end also did I write, that I might know the proof of you, whether ye be obedient in all things.

10 To whom ye forgive any thing, I forgive also: for if I forgave any thing, to whom I forgave it, for your sakes forgave I it in the person of Christ;

11 Lest Satan should get an advantage of us: for we are not ignorant of his devices.

THE MEAL:
WHAT WOULD YOU DO ...

What would you do if you never had to work again? What would you be doing now if you had not gone to school, got that job, or stayed in that relationship? What would you do, if you lost everything? What would you do if you could not fit any of your clothes? What would you eat if you had no food in the house? What would you do if you were in prison without parole? What would you do if you had no voice? What would you do if you could not see? What would you do if no one ever gave you a chance? What would you do, if you never heard the words "I love you?" What would you do if you did not follow your dreams? What would you do if you were disliked? What would you do without an imagination? What would you do for someone else?

Proverbs 16:9 – A man's heart plans his way But the Lord directs his steps.

Proverbs 27:1 – Do not boast about tomorrow, for you do not know what a day may bring forth.

Proverbs 3:5 – Trust in the Lord with all your heart, and lean not on your own understanding.

Psalm 27:13 – I would have lost heart, unless I had believed that I would see the goodness of the Lord in the land of the living.

MINI AUTOBIOGRAPHY

I attended a retreat offered by my church, a few years ago. It was at an exclusive five star, resort and spa in Maryland. It was wonderful! Women of all ages came together to fellowship, relax, and "tell their story". Like so many, my mind started racing. "Okay, the story has to be about me and my life experiences. Well, I could tell a story of how a once Girl Scout, debutant, and college graduate, earned her stripes, while residing in a women's detention facility. But, who would want to hear about that?"

Everyone knows someone who has had some type of run-in with the law. Oh I know, I'll share how I was in a unhealthy relationship with a college boyfriend. Haven't we all had that experience? I guess I can share about a certain group of young women I associated with for a period in my life. They always appeared to enjoy life and had no cares in the world, the flip side was for some odd reason the encounters always lead to something tragic.

I could share how I wasn't focused and dropped out of school. But who would want to hear about these stories? What if I started sharing and no one takes me seriously? Finally, I figured, I'll allow God to guide me in telling the story he wants me to tell.

(The story I would share)

Reflecting on my childhood, in my view, it seemed normal. I was the younger of two children in a single-parent household. My mom was an educator. We were one of a few African-American families living in a predominately white neighborhood where our family endured many trials. The neighborhood expressed by burning cross in our front yard and monthly break-ins that they did not want us there.

I recalled not being allowed to attend classmate sleepovers and being chased to school by older kids who chanted the "N" word and spit on me. But this would not deter the vision my mother had for her children. It was unfortunate that my parents split after purchasing our home. Little did I know that in my season, God would reveal why he selected me and my family to play the main characters in this play of life.

With each life experience or act there is an audience to give the reviews. It is amazing that in some people's eyes, I had it made. I now know that I have to thank God for my life. Even in the midst of the heartache and setbacks, I am fortunate because I am alive and can share my story to encourage someone else. Bingo! I got I, my purpose in life is to tell my story for someone else.

I was this fragile soul in my primary years. I constantly yearned to be with my parents, a.k.a; abandonment issues. I always had a need for one of my parents or sibling to be near. I recall being teased a lot by relatives. No one understood why I was crying or so fearful. As an adult, seeing some of the issues that stemmed from my childhood, has definitely explained my fears.

In our house, we would set goals, play board games, and read books. We attended church and ate over grandma's house on Sunday. At school, we represented black culture through our hair and ethnic names. But around our extended family we had to defend our speech by using proper English and our dress code by wearing Izod, Bermuda shorts, and penny loafers, and why we lived where we lived. That was pressure. I was too young to have this load on my shoulders.

Fun times would come though. We would travel with Amway to different cities and get to swim in hotel pools. Room service was my favorite, though my Mom's facial expression at checkout, implied otherwise. Once in the third grade, I out guessed the entire school, on how many jelly beans were in the jar. I received a $10 gift certificate to the book fair and an award at the school assembly. Thinking BIG paid off!!! I recall one time when, my mother gave me a blank check so I could buy a book from the book fair. Well, I thought I would just go ahead and buy like the whole series by Judy Bloom. I was so excited.

Well, I am just a kid right? Remember that facial expression my mother gave at the check- out from the hotel, well you can only imagine the expression she had when she received that bank statement. See mom, you told me to read!!!! I love you!

Let see, what about those pre-teen days……..
My mom eventually remarried and my sister went away to college. Now, I was at home alone and felt I was on my own in this cruel world. I just couldn't believe my mother. She just loved to make my life miserable. She wanted to know everything and expected me to keep my room clean. She would read my letters and monitored who I was hanging out with. She even had the nerve to get all my friends and their parent's telephone numbers.

I thought, "Believe it or not Mom, I am a good kid. You do not have to worry about me." Oh, I can top this. My Mom made me do all of these things that as a teenager didn't seem cool. I had to make speeches in church, attend modeling/charm school enrichment, volunteer at the events hosted by the committees that my

Mom served on, and had to participate with other youth in activities that embraced my heritage and culture. This was truly the pits! I was trying to figure out how doing all this was going to help me?

Well you are probably thinking, Tosh what was fun for you? I am glad you asked. Talking on the phone to my friends about nothing was fun. Going to the mall with my friends to meet boy was fun. Now I know a lot of my friends may have displayed that they were a little more grown acting than I was. Most parents in my Mom's position would have had me under lock and key. In my teen defense, I was quite vocal on things, which of course did not help in reasoning with my Mom.

Now, here comes high school............
Boys, boys, and more boys. There were concerts, house parties, football games, college parties, and the pressure of making the right decisions. To summarize this chapter in my life, it was a HIT or MISS.

By my senior year, I had dated the most popular boy, partied with the most popular group, and had even been the unpopular girl in some popular settings. Being in the know became my focal point. Can you say social butterfly? Once again, my mother began nagging me about going to college stuff. Duh, I know I'm going to college, even though I had yet to apply. Oh yea, I forgot to mention there is this halo that reads P-R-O-C-R-A-S-T-I-N-A-T-O-R on my forehead.

Due to the halo, I stayed at home and attended a local school,

while all my friends had gone away to out of state universities. I have no one to blame but me. I tell you one thing; I was not going to stay here. I had to break up out of this camp. I knew what was best for me, but I knew my mom would not go for it unless I presented a plan.

I had written out a plan as to why I should move-out and my mother should pay for it. (It worked!!!) My mother honored her end of the deal. Some where in my new found freedom; I did not quite follow through. Can you say breach of contract? After leaving the nest, my actions stated I missed the nest. My mother and step-dad would wake up to find me in my old room. Well, it gets even better. I emotionally and physically dropped out of school. I had a transcript of incompletes to prove it. Thank God I can laugh about it now.

By now I am sure you know Mom's facial expression. So picture the one she was giving at this point. All my being vocal was just that. My mother decided that our next family trip to a wedding would be a long-term stay for me, which was non-negotiable. I took the silent treatment route.

Prior to the move, I had confided in a friend about the school issue. She suggested that I apply as a freshman at the university that she was attending and not even mention the previous year. I did just that. I did not even tell my Mom.

While away on my long-term retreat I found my passion. While staying with relatives, my uncle helped me get an internship working on a bereavement study. I was making money and no one was there to pressure me. This was just what I needed.

Through the summer, my sister would call and be a mediator for conversations between my mother and I. One day I receive a call from my mother. I hadn't heard her sound this pleasant in months. She had received my acceptance letter from the university that I had applied to without her knowledge. I am sure as a parent this was a great feeling after all the stunts I had pulled. There is a God! Not only was I given a chance to redeem myself, I was going off to college to explore life with friends.

I am sure with a lot of prayer and faith; my mother decided that she would sponsor me. Of course I had to keep up my end. If my grades dropped, I was on my own. What do you think happened? Here we go, three thousand miles away with no parental guidance. You would have thought I had learned my lesson, NOT!!!!

Have you ever heard of academic probation? It was written in bold print at the bottom of my report card, which arrived at my parent's home during the winter break. What a Christmas gift. This is where you'd say Tosh, didn't you learn anything? Of course, I learned how to party, drink, party, and take road trips. I did like this school. I will get it together. And I did. I had some moments, but I eventually made honor roll some semesters. So that would conclude that I stop partying. Now that just would not be me.

Throughout my four years of college, I had switched majors. I had been cut-off from my Mom. I experienced my share of heartbreaks and headaches or hangovers, same thing. It is all good. You never know how good you have it until the plug is pulled. I would spend my summers at home taking summer courses, ob-

taining employment, and voluntarily terminating employment. Did I mention that I did party? One summer I made a living out of collecting employment training checks. My mother couldn't say much because she was the one who taught me not to quit unless I had another job. Thank you Mom for the great advice.

Time had passed and I guess I was having too much fun. I was invited to meet with the dean of the department. The dean had reviewed my file and shared that I should not have to stay another semester just for one class. I am the blame. I was granted the privilege of taking the class in another department that summer and I graduated. Hallelujah!

Now what? Due to my previous impulsive decision making, my mother thought she would help me along the way. All I had to do was to give my John Hancock. After the ceremony we drove straight to the post office to send off my registration to take the teaching certification test. I put my Mom on the plane. I thought about her last words, "You have two weeks, love you."

The world I had known for the past four years no longer existed. Like LL Cool J said, "I'm going back to Cali." Now going back to California would not open the doors of opportunity until the baggage of the past was cleared out. Here I was a recent college graduate hoping for a promising career. Apparently I had a" to-do list" before I could even get started.

The childhood gripes I had with my Dad, the habits I had picked up in my independent travels, and the healthy and not so healthy bondages in relationships would soon come into fruition. All that

I had ever been taught experience, or had been blind to would come full circle. We have all endured trials and tribulations. I was going to learn through mine whether voluntarily or not.

Things were looking good. I had started the healing process through on-going communication with my father. I was working and renting an apartment with a friend from high school. I was not partying as often. As far as I could see I was maturing. (Tunnel vision) Well, not quite. A while back I may have mentioned how I enjoyed partying with friends. Since I was doing so well, I wanted to celebrate by having an evening on the town with friends. It was as normal of a night than any other. I believe I also mentioned that some encounters ended tragically. Well, this was one of those nights. There may have been a brawl or words with other groups of girls before but this time it was tad bit different. This night it was between me and one of my friends.

This was the test of my life. I would now be accountable for what I had said or done. It was a process. What was considered a punishment was actually a blessing in disguise. I was sent on a retreat. I love retreats. It is like detoxing self of whatever is toxic to my system. Of course I did not like my new place of residence. There were no luxuries. But for my birthday, I got to watch Oprah!!! That was the best gift. I exercised, meditated, read a lot, attended church, and wrote in my journal daily. I even learn how to sew. That was real good for me. Of course it was easy to put everything in perspective.

Even there, I had dealt with the same or similar experiences that I just could not seem to get right on my own in the communication

department. As of today, all individuals involved in the specified event are living their lives as I am. If any harm was meant by either party, whether intentional or not, God prevailed. I have made amends and paid my debts to society. I know the God I trust and believe in is a God of second chances.

I have moved into a new phase. I have embarked on new relationships, ventures, and just life. It has been eight years. I am finally teaching, a new homeowner, an active member of my church, volunteer for the homeless, still reading, occasional travel without the room service, and I speak to my mother daily. Oh yeah, did I mention that my Dad is in the picture?

Throughout my short years on this earth, I have learned a lot but I know I still have so much more to learn. It is important to listen and pay attention. It is important to live and learn what it is you are called to do. I guess I do have a story to tell after all.

www.ingramcontent.com/pod-product-compliance
Lightning Source LLC
Chambersburg PA
CBHW022113280326
41933CB00007B/370